In Defense of Lifting up Jesus: WILL YOU STAND IN THE GAP WITH ME?

In Defense of Lifting up Jesus: WILL YOU STAND IN THE GAP WITH ME?

Wanda Treadway

Order this book online at www.trafford.com
or email orders@trafford.com

Most Trafford titles are also available at major online book retailers.

Printed in the United States of America.

ISBN: 978-1-4269-7555-4 (sc)
ISBN: 978-1-4269-7556-1 (e)

Trafford rev. 07/20/2011

 www.trafford.com

North America & International
toll-free: 1 888 232 4444 (USA & Canada)
phone: 250 383 6864 ♦ fax: 812 355 4082

Dedication

This book is dedicated to the Holy Spirit

Jesus said, "Nevertheless I tell you the truth;

It is expedient for you that I go away; for if I

go not away, the Comforter will not come unto

you; but if I depart, I will send him unto you."

_____ John 15:7

CONTENTS

Acknowledgements

_____ To my sister Marvetta, thanks for your support, and reading and editing every chapter in my book. I couldn't have written this book without your honesty, even when I thought you were hard on me. But when my book is published, we'll both be blessed for lifting up Jesus!

_____ To Johnnie Travis, my Publishing Consultant at Trafford Publishing, because of your heeding the Holy Spirit to contact me fourteen years later, I am publishing my book In Defense of Lifting up Jesus: Will You Stand In The Gap With Me? All because you believed in me, and where ever you are, may the Lord continue to bless you, and I will always be grateful to you.

_____ To Gail Glenn, my editor, thanks for being the driving force for me writing this book, because of your enthusiasm and love for the Lord, I stayed motivated to complete my manuscript. Again thanks for your help and support, and may the Lord continue to bless you.

_____ A special thanks to House of David Ministries, for accepting me into the Aspiring Ministers' Program. As a result of, faithfully doing the weekly assignments, I have learned that I can be a vessel for God. What's more, I am learning to "rightly divide God's Word" and be on the lookout for false teachers who ever and where ever; they may be.

_____ To my mentors for life, I would like to thank Professor Joanne Isbey who taught me to edit and re-edit my work. To my first English teacher at Rouge Academy at Ford's, I would like to thank Barb for believing in me and encouraging me to keep writing; even though I wasn't good at it. In addition, to my other teacher, John thanks for all your patience and reading my chapters for my first book titled Farrakhan: The God I Serve Is Not A Silk Salesman that I wrote in 1997. As it worked out, 14 years later, I am publishing my book first book! So wherever all of you are, I love you and may God bless you and your families.

_____ To my pastor, Superintend Tommy C. Vanover l, Pastor, Glory To Glory Temple. I would like to thank-you for heeding Psalms 12:6-7, "The words of the Lord are pure words: as silver tried in a furnace of earth, purified seven times." Because of this, God's Word is not to be watered down, but preach the way the Lord intended his servants to preach with power, and "He Will Draw All Men."

_____ To Evangelist, Vivian M.Vanover, First Lady Glory To Glory Temple. Without a doubt, you are truly a woman of God, and hearing you speak at West Willow's 33rd Annual Woman's Day Program, left me with this conclusion, "Lord, bless me, with her tenacity, passion and spirit—for the furtherance of the Lord's kingdom." Amen

_____ To my Dad, to hear him said that I am "On fire and full of joy" shows how the Holy Spirit is pricking his heart and showing my Dad that Jesus can turn man around, even when his heart is hearten that he can change when he accepts and believes in Him. Thank-you, Jesus.

_____ To my mother, thanks I needed to hear these words, "Wanda, you are going into spiritual battle," yes I am. For this reason, I am putting on the whole armor of God, to fend off the fiery darts of the wicked.

_____ To my daughter, Clarice and my four year old grand-daughter, Brelyn I am leaving you my legacy a book that takes a stance for Jesus, because He loved us first. As for me and my house, we will serve the One and only true God---Jesus Christ. Furthermore, my prayer is that you will raise your daughter the same way; I raised you, to love the Lord with all your heart and soul. In addition, the fear of the Lord is the beginning of wisdom; remember this always!

_____ To my sister-in-law, Iris thanks for loving me enough to share the Good News of the Gospel with me. Because when I was in my late twenties, I wasn't thinking about getting saved. But, because of you witnessing to me a unrepentant sinner, I accepted Jesus Christ, as my personal Savior. What's more, looking back over my life and where God has brought me from, I'm grateful to you because you didn't want me to end up in the fiery pits of Hell!

_____ Most importantly, I want to thank the Holy Spirit for helping me write this book. Especially because every night before I went to sleep, the Holy Spirit would give me what to write for each chapter of my book, the titles of every chapter, what websites to use, and what Scriptures to use in the Bible. Without a doubt, I am certain, that without the Holy Spirit's guidance, I could not have written this book. Because He told me, "If You Lift Me Up, I Will Draw All Men." In closing, Lord it's my prayer same as Jabez in the book entitled The Prayer of JABEZ, that you will increase my territory, and 'Your Will Be Done; and not mine's.

PREFACE

In Defense Of Lifting Up Jesus:
Will You Stand In the Gap With Me?

To begin with,
my reasons for writing this book.

While listening to my favorite radio ministry The Journey with Pastor Ron Moore, he was talking about Ron Bell's book "Love Wins" but it was when he mention the word 'toxic' in the same sentence, it was then that I started paying attention to what Moore was sharing with his radio audience. It seems the religious community was caught off guard by Ron Bell's comparing the Jesus story an essential truth of the Christian faith as being "misguided and toxic." [1]

It was hearing these words about Jesus' message of love and forgiveness considered as toxic, that upset me so bad, I felt compelled to write my own book. More importantly, I wrote this book, because the Holy Spirit told me it was time, and lead me to this scripture in God's Word saying, "And I sought for a man among them, that should make up the hedge and stand in the gap before me the Lord . . ." Ezekiel 22:30

Firstly, because I do not agree with Ron Bell's theology, as it related to how he interprets or misinterprets God's Word in his book Love Wins: A Book About Heaven, Hell, And The Fate of Every Person Who Ever Lived. It seems, Pastor Bell has chosen to "lean to his own understanding" and for a man of the cloth,

I found this rather disturbing! Especially when a lot of peoples lives are hanging in the balance and because Jesus was killed for much less, for telling the truth—so that man would live and not pine away in the Bermuda Triangle of hell!

Secondly, these are the other things I found frustrating about Ron Bell's book in my opinion, he takes key scriptures out of context, dares to challenge God's authority on topics ranging from salvation, heaven, hell, but what irked me the most, pointing fingers at the Jesus story. For suddenly, I realized the Body of Christ was not on 'One Accord' and to quote John Macarthur,[2] these words sums up why Christians everywhere — Should Stand In the Gap For Jesus!

> "We Who Love Christ And Believe
> The Truth Embodied In His Teachings
> Must Awaken To The Reality Of The Battle
> That Is Raging All Around Us."

Thirdly, who are the other Jesuses, Ron Bell keeps referring to in his book? Is it The World Church, in Revelation, The Antichrist, or Baal in the Old Testament? For in the preface, to quote Bell, "So when we hear that a certain person has "rejected Christ," we should first ask, 'Which Christ?" Even more puzzling he goes on to speak about the 'real' Jesus, what does he mean the real Jesus? There's only one who is real? The Bible God's word only speaks of one, and it's as if Bell is attempting re dress the historical Jesus! So is he guilty, of not adhering to the Word of God, and the teachings Jesus taught His disciples, and not spreading Jesus' message of hope? Or does Bell's theology instills in his followers a negative and" forced orthodoxy?"[3] Especially as it pertains to pushing his agenda on man, instead of doing God's will which is to; save humanity instead of luring them into the fiery furnace of hell!

The purpose of this book is to inform readers and Christians that society at large, has chosen not only to make the historical

Jesus, in the Bible a scapegoat for what ills society. But, even the apostates in the church they are trying to replace the God-man Jesus, turning Him into the "Eucharistic Christ"[4] in my opinion, a ritual; similar to worshipping Baal and never having a personal relationship with him, unlike the relationship Christians have with Jesus Christ, my Lord and Savior!

But what does all this mean? Man no longer will interested in seeking Jesus' invitation to receive His 'free gift of salvation,' instead they have chosen another god the Eucharist; a communion performed in Catholic churches. Which is entirely different from communion Christians are accustomed to doing in remembrance of Christ Jesus, who made the ultimate sacrifice for humanity— spilled His precious blood, a innocent lamb slaughtered, crucified unjustly, and killed by men in long flowing priestly robes — that we would not be slaves; of the Devil!

Chapter 1

"In Defense of Lifting Up Jesus"
Will You Stand In the Gap With Me?

Man Has Always Made the Wrong Choice, and Rob Bell Is No Different!

"Who concerning the truth have erred . . . and overthrow the faith of some"

II Timothy 2:18, 19

To err is human, to forgive is divine, oh the beauty of these words taken from Alexander Pope's Essay on Criticism. In this case, this quote definitely applies to Pastor Rob Bell's criticism of the Jesus Story; which he unjustifiably has blown out of proportion. Pastor Bell's perspective and criticism of the Jesus Story deliberately chooses to plant seeds of doubt instead of seeds of hope, and reminds me of the parable of the sower. The perspective of Pastor Bell, in relation to the Jesus Story, is not unique as there have been numerous times that the Jesus Story has been tossed out with the baby's bath water; and scripturally hijacked. Pastor Bell is only another man with the aim of, as II Timothy 2:19 says, to "overthrow the faith of some" and to mislead the saved as well as the unsaved, making it harder for them to come to grips with the truth surrounding the birth of

Jesus and his life story, on which the foundation of Christianity is built.

It appears that, Mr. Bell is not a true believer of the Christian faith and this saddens me. On behalf of the "2.1 billion Christians" (www.adherents.com) along with persecuted Christians around the globe that take the Jesus story seriously, we find Rob Bell's Theology flawed and extremely toxic! Obviously, Pastor Bell has not heard of the infamous Rev. Richard Wurmbrand (1909-2001), founder of Voice of the Martyrs (VOM), who spent 14 torturous years in Romanian hell like prisons. Rev. Richard Wurmbrand served his prison sentence alongside the many persecuted adherents of whom were literally being burned at the stake daily, but yet despite this persecution, are holding fast to their faith all because of their faith in the validity of the Jesus Story. Being crucified daily and in spite of these blasphemous dictators attempting through persecution to diminish the beacon of light that they carry around in their hearts. It is their unrelenting faith in the Jesus Story that allows them to take being physically and mentally tortured, holding steadfast against being spiritually raped of their beliefs.

These persecuted Christians truly understand what it means to walk in Jesus' footprints! Surely, Pastor Bell has forgotten what it means to "stand in the gap for Jesus" the Bible says, "When one person in the Body of Christ suffers, we all suffer." In lieu of this, it's understandable why the Christian community is crying afoul at Pastor Rob Bell's hinting that the Christian faith is "toxic". This particular belief of Pastor Bell's is "toxic" to Christians in third world countries that are being killed for just having a Bible and are considered traitors by their own governments, and are being stoned for serving a God, in whom their government do not believe in. In contrast to the persecuted Christians there are some Christians that have religious freedom, in this great country, that share the same perspective on the Jesus Story as Pastor Bell.

God give us an explanation for this kind of unbelief in II Timothy 2: 18-19, "Who concerning the truth has erred . . . and overthrown the faith." Based on the guidance of scripture, it is no doubt in my belief that in Pastor Bell's case his concepts on the Jesus Story is indicative of this scripture and attempts to overthrow the Christian faith by discrediting Jesus, who is the foundation of Christianity. As I contemplated what faith really means to Christianity the Holy Spirit spoke to my spirit guiding me to read II Timothy 2:19, "Nevertheless, the foundation of God standeth sure, having this seal, The Lord knoweth them that are His. And, let everyone that nameth the name of Christ depart from iniquity." After reading this scripture, I was not distraught anymore because of Pastor Bell's conviction on the concept of the Jesus Story. Scripture speaks of the "coming apostasy" as mention in II Timothy 3:1-5, "For in the last days perilous times shall come and men shall blasphemers, unholy, false accusers, and more importantly lovers of pleasures more than lovers of God; having a form of godliness, but denying the power thereof from such turning away."

As the Lord enlightened my upstanding, I thought "that's it" Lord, our concept of Christianity, unlike Pastor Bell's pseudo religion, is based on the solid foundation of Jesus Christ our Lord and Savior. It was then the Holy Spirit guided me to another scripture, St. Matthew 7:24, "No man can serve two masters: for either he will hate the one, and love the other; or else he will hold to the one, and despise the other. Ye cannot serve God and mammon." I thanked the Holy Spirit for directing me to these biblical verses. Satan, the "Grand Deceiver", has once again deceived the elect by twisting the concept of the word of God in Pastor Bell's mind, I mused to myself. As fellow Christians ask yourselves this one fundamental question, whose theology is toxic; our Lord's or Pastor Bell's? It is false theology, such as Pastor Bell's and numerous other false preachers that determines a man's fate and ultimately plays a part in determining whether an individual goes to heaven or spend eternity in the *'Hot Zone'----a Wi Fi Hot Spot in Hell!* The preaching of false theology is not unique and this is not the first or last time That the Jesus Story will subject to attempts to be devoured by ravenousness wolves. But remember, fellow believers in Christ, that the time of false preachers and their "theology" shall also pass.

With the uttermost respect to Christ Jesus, my Lord and Savior, Christians worldwide embrace the Jesus Story as the most pivotal events to ever occur in the history of Christianity. Jesus is our only hope, a beacon of light, in these perilous times in today's godless society. On the basis of this, the Jesus story, along with the good news of the Gospel, gives us hope and I do not believe statements that Christians view the Jesus story as "toxic". It is my belief that Christians take consolation in the words of the apostle Paul for "our faith is not in vain". The message of sacrifice, love, hope and forgiveness learned from the story of Jesus reminds Christians that they will inherit the gift of eternal life through salvation, which is based on the belief in Jesus Christ as being our Redeemer. In contrast to this, it is the goal of Antichrist like theories that try to persuade Christians to be misled and inadvertently cause them to worship a "counterfeit" God that fits their concept of an "acceptable" man based theology!

As it stands Jesus is recognized in all cultures and religions, even though they are separate or clearly different from Christianity, their cultures recognize Jesus as a prophet. Christianity spans as far back as the days of Caesar, and continues to strive in the heart and souls of Christians all over the world today. So, can the Emerging Church Movement Supporters compete with Jesus of Nazareth, the founder of Christianity? And although an exclusive group of emergent pastors have begun to jump on the "Christians are crazy" Bandwagon, Christianity still stands. In my opinion I believe that some of these emergent pastors, in particular Pastor Bell, are guilty of down grading the validity of Jesus to appear as a fleeting silk sales man; offering his wares to a particular group of people willing to buy into His stories. This ridiculously absurd concept is furthest from the truth!

Christians chose their faith on the basis of a rock solid biblical and historical foundation in our Lord and Savior, Jesus Christ.

As far as Pastor Bell is concerned only a select few who believe in the Jesus Story will be accepted into the fold; providing that they accept rather his version of theology, instead of the traditional path to salvation. The belief in Jesus and the biblical and historical account of His life, in entirety, is paramount to Christianity.

According to Pastor Bell's theology a spiteful Jesus will toss those Christians that do not follow his concept of theology into Purgatory, never being ushered through the pearly gates. Has Pastor Bell ever heard of, the biblical words that clearly state, "Thou Mayst?" A simple interpretation of these words is that God gives us all the ability to choose between good and evil! It would seem that an biblically righteous man of the cloth, would shroud his loins with God's word, but alas this does not always appear to be the case with some of the spiritual leaders today. The scripture instructs us on this very issue when encountering prophets that lean towards "their own" understanding, but yet prophesize in the name of our Lord:

Matthew 7: 21 – 23

> Many will say to me on that day, 'Lord, Lord, did we not prophesy in your name, and in your name drive out demons and perform many miracles?' Then I will tell them plainly, 'I never knew you. Away from me, you evildoers!

There is every reason to conclude that the absurdity of Pastor's Bell's theology is that his particular belief lacks hope for the billions of Christians whose faith hinges on the Jesus story. It is due to this type of "man based" theology that many followers of Christ Jesus just may find Pastor Bell's choice of words regarding Christian beliefs (Toxic) as being offensive, especially coming from a man of the cloth! Surely, many followers of Christ, who know His voice and share my sentiments that the only thing that Christians might find "toxic" is the theology of Pastor Bell.

Corinthians 11:13 –

"For such are false prophets, deceitful workers, transforming themselves into the apostles of Christ.

Chapter 2

Leaning To one's Own Understanding Is this the New Paradigm: When Teaching God's Word?

" . . . Lean not unto thine own understanding,
and be not wise in thine own eyes . . ."

Proverbs 3: 5, 8

It is God's Word the Scriptures, that forms the basis of man's religious beliefs, and not the teachings [for] doctrines the commandments of men" (Matthew 15:9) which Jesus said undeniably, leads to hypocrisy. For *Jesus* points this out in Mark 7:8 *"For laying aside the commandments of God, ye hold the traditions of men, [as] the washing of pots and cups: and many other such like things ye do,"* and He also reiterates that the reason for this, is so man can *"Full well ye reject the commandments of God, that ye may keep your own tradition."* If we travel through time during the era of the Pharisees, the religious men of Jesus day, we will see that they also were guilty of leaning to their own understanding as it relates to what they choose to teach the people versus God's commandments and what was scripturally correct, and adding doctrine that wasn't ordained by God! As an illustration, the Pharisees were teaching tradition and commandments of men as doctrine such as the "washing hands (ceremonially) before eating, that they considered a sacred ritual and in reality, they were teaching it as doctrine."[5]

On the basis of this, Jesus found the Pharisees on the wrong side of the law and Titus 2:14 explains that they were " . . . giving heed to Jewish fables, and commandments of men, that turn away from the truth" in order that they may please themselves; rather than God! There is every reason to conclude, not only . . . but also, the Pharisees were in the wrong; they were at fault of teaching traditions and commandments of men as doctrine "can their traditions be on par with God's word?"[6]

According to Tony Warren's web article The Doctrine of Sola Scriptura: Is it really Biblical? In order for the Pharisees in Jesus' day traditions to be on par with God's word "the one speaking it would have to be either God, or the very least be equal to God, and the only other alternatives are to be receiving revelations direct from God or to be "quoting" God testifying or witnessing faithfully."[7] Clearly, they were not doing that, for "just as it wouldn't be for vain traditions that the Pharisees held that Jesus condemned because their traditions had made the word of God of non-effect."[8] Thinking about the Pharisees in Jesus' day, I was reminded that false teachers have been with us, since the beginning of time and today's generation isn't any different, for there are many pastors and servants of the Lord who "are unruly and vain talkers and deceivers and whose mouths must be stopped who mislead whole houses, teaching things which they ought not, for filthy lucre's sake." (Titus 1: 10, 11) I cried out, "Lord, not only are these false teachers misleading whole households, their misleading millions through the internet, satellites, and cable!" All of a sudden, I remembered the 60 Minutes segment that Bryon Pitts had with popular television evangelist, Joel Osteen whose latest book "Become A Better You" and focuses on seven principles he believes will improve their lives, to believe in yourself, build better relationships, and embrace the place where you are. That's good for self improvement, but I agree with Byron Pitts on 60 Minutes that there's "Not one mention of God or not one mention of Jesus Christ"[9] anywhere in the book, and Osteen got a whooping $13 million advance for the book, and on top of that, it was number one on the New York Times bestseller list! And I wondered, if this qualifies as "filthy lucre" and the Bible refers to is as ill-gotten money!" (Titus 1:11) What's more, Osteen believes these seven principles will improve individuals' lives, but to quote Osteen "that's just my message and there is scripture in there that backs it all up, and these are principles that can help you, and I don't think (scriptures) that's my gifting."[10] So I was unsure, "What is Osteen's gift the gift of gab?" And Does Joel Osteen teachings fall into the category of a tradition of man? And will keep people from establishing a personal relationship with Jesus, because having a positive self image is a lot different than having a personal relationship with God, and besides the focus is on good works, and Galatians 2:16 says just the opposite "Knowing that a man is not justified by the works of the law, but the faith of Jesus Christ . . . for by the works of the law shall no flesh be justified, and by grace are ye saved through faith; and that not of yourselves: it is the gift of God: Not of works, lest any man should boast." (Ephesians 2:8, 9) Are you listening Joel Osteen, for the Lord says, "If ye continue in my word, then are ye my disciples indeed; And ye shall know the truth, and the truth shall make you free." (John 8:31, 32) As I was reflecting on Osteen's book that "Become A Better You" which is a bestseller, I was thinking is he boasting?

Because to me it was heartbreaking, surely Osteen's book instructs people to abide by man's traditions, instead of obeying the commandments of God!" In comparison, the traditions of Joel Osteen that he details in his book "Become A Better You" can be considered as being created in "sophistry after the principles of the world, and not after Christ."[11] Because of this, Christians are to heed Colossians 2; 8, and to "Beware lest any man spoil you through philosophy and vain deceit, after the tradition of men, after the rudiments of the world, and not after Christ." For according to Tony Warren these traditions of men are "patterned after the imaginations of self-justification, cannot be laid at the feet of God or put in His mouth divine precepts."[12] I wonder if Osteen was doing this with his best selling book. "After all he never even mention God or Jesus' name once—is this cause for self-justification or not!" The Holy Spirit descended upon me "There is a way that seemeth right unto a man, but the end thereof are the ways of death." (Proverbs 16:25) Unfortunately, many in the church-world in today's generation are leaning unto their "own understanding" placing their own heart's desires above the scriptures . . . instead of God's word in the Bible"[13] As always I thanked the Holy Spirit for helping me to see that although "there is a way that seemth right unto a man, but the end thereof are the ways of death." (Proverbs 16:25)

This is the reverse of, what the Scriptures teach for "in all matters of faith and practice the Holy Bible is a Christian's only safety net, and it is the authority by which we should *"judge righteous judgment"* and discern between the righteous and the wicked, between him that serveth God and him that served him not"[14] Hence, it's no secret that Rev. Michael Horton, a professor of theology at Westminster Seminary in Escondido, Calif. 'think it's a cotton candy gospel" and he went on to explain that "His core message is God is nice, you're nice, be nice," and "He uses the Bible like a fortune cookie. 'This is what's gonna happen for you. There's gonna a windfall in your life tomorrow.'[15] The Bible's not meant to be read that way.' Well, Holy Spirit also in this same interview on 60 Minutes Bryon Pitts tells Joel Osteen "But many theologians from mainstream churches find your message misleading and shallow."[16]

Chapter 3

False Teachers: Not adhering to phrase "Sola Scriptura"

"But there were false prophets also among the people, even as there shall be false teachers among you, who privily shall bring in damnable heresies, even denying the Lord that brought them, and bring upon themselves swift destruction. And many shall follow their pernicious; by reasons of whom the way of truth shall be evil spoken of."

2 Peter 2:1-2

Matthew 24:11 says "And many false prophets shall rise, and shall deceive many" unfortunately this a sign of the times that we live in today for Christians and the Church, for many false teachers are guilty of "actively seeking unity on the basis of (supernatural) manifestations, many times at the expense of doctrinal truth"[17] as a consequence, these false teachers aren't living up to their sense of duty to "draw nigh unto God" (James 4:8) and instead are choosing to lean to their own understanding as it relates to sharing God's Word as stated in the Bible, with their congregations. It seems, certain pastors are not "taking heed to the precepts of the Word of God"[18] for if they took the Bible seriously and were rooted in the Word of Truth (*The Bible*) they would realize that "doctrine is the key to discernment and fighting deception."[19] Furthermore, false teachers are not adhering to the "Doctrine of Sola Scriptura" but unlike Christians in the Reformation Church era took the position that the Bible was God's wholly inspired word, and as such was the "sole infallible" rule of faith and practice for the Church."[20] In fact, numerous pastors in today's churches consider the word of God to be run of the mill or nothing special, and refuse to accept the word of God as the utmost authority that man must follow. However, this is not happening, because man has chosen to not be obedient and he certainly has not put his trust in God's laws but rather in: self-belief! The Lord said to me, "Wanda, do you remember King Josiah in the Old Testament?" I replied, "No, I'm not familiar with the Old Testament Lord." The Lord answered, "Well, you should be!" So I got my Bible and looked up 2nd Kings 22:10-13 and discovered that the Hil-ki-ah the high priest and the scribe Sha-phan had found the book of the law in the house of the Lord. And the scribe showed the book to King Josiah of Judah, which high priest had given him, and it came to pass, when the King had heard the words of the book, he immediately tore off his clothes. "It was as if, his clothes were like dirty rags unto the Lord" and he commanded both the priest and the scribe to go inquire of the Lord for him, and for the people of all Judah, concerning the words of this book that is found: for great is the wrath of the Lord that is kindled against us, because our fathers have not hearkened unto the words of this book, to do according unto all that which is written . . ." After reading 2nd Kings 22:10-13, I understood why the Holy Spirit had me read these verses, for today's pastors are not adhering to the "Scripture solely or to the "scriptures alone" and there must be a restoration of the laws of God," [21] for in our time, we are seeing a falling away (*apostasy*) in the midst of the church! For unlike King Josiah, various pastors have chosen to neglect God's Word and in doing so, are causing their adherents to be disobedient, for their shepherds' eyes are not open and they obviously are not concerned about restoring their congregations to previous obedience, so that they can be in right standing with God! Thinking to myself, "Lord, being your faithful servant, I can not rest on my laurels and do nothing that's why I'm writing about false teachers, because based on the doctrine of Sola Scriptura, the Scriptures are the greatest gift God gave man, and come from the highest authority and cannot be overruled by; mere men!

More importantly, false teachers are not in tune with Psalms 12:6-7 for "The words of the Lord are pure words: as silver tried in a furnace of earth, purified seven times" or they would without a doubt, "keep them, O Lord, and thou shall preserve them from this generation for ever." On the basis of these two scriptures alone, they would take the phrase "Sola scriptura" in a true or literal way, without adding false details or deceit to God's flawless word, for the "Holy Cannon contains all that is necessary for Christian faith"[22] besides words to live by today! There comes a time, and that time is now, that no matter how trustworthy a Christian believes their Church leaders may be in teaching his flock for they are still mortal, and can be carnal minded and not be lead by the Holy Spirit, resulting in their theology being inconsistent, and not biblically correct! So, regardless of what the Christian has been taught, you must understand that is central to our faith that the "only infallible "source" for truth is God, and beside God Himself, only His Holy words (the Scriptures alone) are infallible, and shall be preserved forever for man."[23] Because of this, Christians should heed Psalm 149:6-9, "that it is written, this honor has all the saints: Praise ye the Lord" and heed John 4:23, "But the hour cometh, and now is, when the true worshippers shall worship the Father in spirit and in truth: for the Father seeketh such to worship him. Also knowing that Believers in Jesus Christ should be assured that " . . . ye shall know the truth, and the truth shall make you free. (John 8:32) Or otherwise, you are denying the Word of God, the Bible, and if you do, you are guilty of denying the One that died on the Cross for you—Jesus, who is "full of grace and truth" (John 1:14) and " . . . whom the world cannot receive, because it seeth him not, neither knoweth him: but ye know him; for he dwelleth with you, and shall be in you. (John14:17)

There is every indication that false teachers in the church, have abused the spiritual gifts God have given them for "carnal, political, or social gain"[24] (II Corinthians 10:3-6) for this reason, God instructs the Christian to use the whole armor of God because it is quicker than a two-edged sword and used in faith— is good for pulling down the demonic strongholds of false teachers and the Devil; whose aim is to corrupt the minds of followers of Christ Jesus; so they will not only believe in Him— but not follow him as well! For this reason, Christians are to remember the words of the Apostle Paul to "contend for the faith" and it's crucial they remember that "For we wrestle not against flesh and blood but against principalities and against powers and against the rulers of the darkness of this world, (Ephesians 6:12) . . . wherefore take unto you the whole armour of God, that ye may be able to withstand in the evil day, and having done all, to stand." (Ephesians 6:13) Similarly, it is vital to the Christians' faith that "Above all, taking the shield of faith, wherewith, ye shall be able to quench all the fiery darts of the wicked" (Ephesians 6:16) which is "the helmet of salvation, and the sword of the Spirit, and the word of God"[25] and stand therefore, having your loins grit about with truth, and having on the breastplate of righteousness." (Ephesians 6:14) Lastly, false teachers are not heeding the Scriptures that "All scripture is given by inspiration of God and is profitable for doctrine, for reproof, for correction, for instruction in righteousness; that the man of God may be perfect, thoroughly furnished unto all good works." (2 Timothy 3:16-17)[26] On the contrary, all church leaders, pastors, and ministers are to heed II Timothy 4:2-4 to "Preach the word; be instant in season, out of season; reprove, rebuke, exhort with all longsuffering and doctrine, for the time will come when they (*false teachers*) they will not endure sound doctrine; but after their own lusts shall they heap to themselves teachers, having itching ears; and they shall turn away their ears from the truth, and shall be turned unto fables." I thanked the Holy Spirit for enlightening me about false teachers "Although personally I have not been shepherded by any, for my pastor is a man after God's own heart—another David!" But suddenly my thoughts turned to Rob Bell, who wrote Love Wins and I couldn't help but remember how he felt about the numerous versions of the Jesus story, going on to say that it "caused those everywhere, who have heard some version of the Jesus story had caused their pulse to rise, their stomach to churn, and their heart to utter those resolute words, "I would never be a part of that."[27] My reply to him is, "It's obvious you did not read 2nd Timothy 4:2-4, or you would be familiar with this scripture, because the Jesus story that you don't want to be a part of is not a parable. Because after all, you stated that "Jesus responds to almost every question he's asked with . . . a question. "What Do you think? How do you read it?" he asks, again and again and again."[28] So my question to Rob is do you believe in the Doctrine of Sola Scriptura? Especially since it is "necessary and essential to true Christianity and is the difference between God's divinely inspired traditions and ordinances, and man made traditions and ordinances."[29]

So the question your flock should be asking you is whether or not your teachings are fables— because God's Word in II Timothy 4:4 says otherwise! With that said, "I wonder if Rob Bell's title suits him, because it seems, in the end his book is really about his fate, and how he understand and chooses to interpret God's Word (*The Scriptures*) concerning Heaven, Salvation, and Hell, or whether everybody that read his book was mislead; because of his skewed take on the Scriptures! "Maybe he should reproof and read Matthew 21:42, 44 for Jesus saith unto them," *Did ye never read in the scriptures,*

the Stone which the builders rejected,
the same is become the head of the corner:
this is the Lord's doing, and it is marvelous in our eyes!"

Verse 21:44

"And whosoever shall fall on this stone shall be broken: but on whomever it shall fall, it will grind him to powder."

And I wondered, "If that was worst than going to Hell!" *And the Lord's last words were "*. . . *and take him away, and cast him into outer darkness: there shall be weeping, and gnashing of teeth."* (Matthew 22:13) No wonder, the Lord said that *"For many are called, but few are chosen.* (Matthew 22:14) As closed my eyes to go to sleep, all I could think about was "I pray that I am called and am amongst the chosen!"

Chapter 4

The Holy Spirit Reveals Himself: Where He's Welcome

"But ye shall receive power, after that the Holy Ghost is come upon you . . ."

_____Acts1:8 (A)

After reading Rob Bell's Book Love Wins: About Heaven, Hell, And The Fate Of Every Person Who Ever Lived, I don't recall him once mentioning anything about the Holy Spirit. "No wonder, I did not feel the Holy Spirit's presence when I read his book" because the Bible says, "the natural man receiveth not the things of the Spirit of God: for they are fooliness unto him: neither can he know them, because they are spirituality discerned." (I Corinthians 2:14)

It seems, Rob Bell ignored I Corinthians 4:16, " . . . that the Spirit of God dwelleth in you?" perhaps, this is why the Holy Spirit and the Jesus story are viewed as a spook; to him! I thought about the word spook and thought about it long and hard, "The Holy Sprit a ghostly figure— Nay, no way! After all, the Holy Sprit reveals Himself to Christians and you can see him at work in Sunday Church services and when individuals change their lives for the better, it's because of the Holy Spirit! The Holy Spirit is real; I had not attended Sunday services for two Sundays, because I was writing my book. But I missed being in God's House and I when to church on the 14th of May, and the Holy Spirit descended upon me while the choir was singing Victory Is Mine's, Victory today is mine's and I told Satan get thee behind for joy is mine's, and the tears began to flow, for the Holy Spirit had touched my heart! And when I looked up the usher, Crystal was handing me a tissue and she said, 'The Holy Spirit has touched your heart." And indeed, He had!

There are many reasons, the Holy Spirit will not reveal Himself and I thought about Pastor Rob Bell's book, thinking, "Maybe it's because he is vain or he has a gigantic ego." It was if a light bulb had come on in my head the Holy Spirit will not reveal Himself; to non believers! I wonder if Rob Bell is a believer. And Pastor Tim Wirth commented saying, "Rob is a great communicator but is he a godly communicator? ""I don't believe so.""[30] To add to this, the Lord gave me another scripture to look up Ephesians 4:17-18, " . . . That ye henceforth walk not as other Gentiles walk, in the vanity of their mind, (emptiness) having the understanding darkened, being alienated from the life of God through the ignorance that is in them, because of the blindness of their heart." Suddenly, the Holy Spirit descended upon me, read John 17:13, for it is evident from Jesus' command to his disciples to baptize "in the Name of the Father, Son, and Holy Ghost" (Matthew 28:19), and to them that believe "But ye shall receive power, after that the Holy Ghost is come upon you . . ." (Acts 1:8) Again the Holy Spirit came to me, "Read Genesis1:26." I replied, "That's the Creation Story; the creation of heaven and earth" (Genesis 1:1) was the Lord showing me something that I had missed, " . . . And the Spirit of God moved upon the face of the waters." (Genesis 1:2) After reading these Scriptures in the Bible, it was as if the Holy Spirit was showing me that God, Son, and the Holy Spirit have been together since the beginning of time!

In opposition, I sense that Pastor Bell possesses the same attitude as the Romans in Jesus' day, and the Apostle Paul referred to this as the "Judaists" attitude, because the Romans also refused to accept the truth about Jesus. To quote Paul, "nor do they burn with interest in the truth; instead they burned with opposition to the truth." Because of this, the Holy Spirit will not reveal himself to carnal minded men. As a result, I Corinthians 3:3 said, "For ye are yet carnal: for whereas there is among you envying, and strife, and divisions, are ye not carnal, and walk as men?

More importantly, Christians agree with the scripture Peter 3:18," For Christ also hath once suffered for sins, the just for the unjust, that he might bring us to God, being put to death in the flesh, but quickened by the Spirit." For this reason, Christians must heed Ephesians 5:18 (A) rein rates that Christians are given "a command to be filled with the Spirit" and admonish us " . . . but be filled with the Spirit." Why you might ask, because the Scriptures tell us "What?

Know ye not that your body is the temple of the Holy Ghost which is in you, which ye have of God, and ye are not you own."(Corinthians 6:19) As I prepared for bed the Lord referred me to these scriptures Romans 8:16."The Spirit itself beareth witness with our spirit, that we are the children of God." While reading Romans 8:11, and immediately I was reminded of the Jesus story, "But if the Spirit of him that raised up Jesus from the dead dwell in you, he that raised up Christ from the dead shall also quicken your mortal bodies by his Spirit that dwelleth in you." For it was if the Holy Spirit was reading my mind, and wanted me to know that He understood why I felt the way I did about Rob Bell's book, but He also told me not to be to hard on him because he reminded me that— that if you Lift Me Up, I Will draw all men; including a dogmatic pastor.

In the simplest terms, the Holy Spirit reveals Himself to them that believe, because "To be filled with the Holy Spirit is to be Spirit-possessed, Spirit-empowered, Spirit-led and Spirit-controlled,"[31] and the Holy Spirit shows up when Christians exhibit faith and acknowledge Him! In addition, Ephesians 4:13 says it all,"Til we all come in the unity of the faith, and of the knowledge of the Son of God, unto a perfect man . . . the Holy Spirit will cease to exist."

Hence, all you will get from religion is more religion, and the real reason for going to church is to worship God— not man. To quote Pastor Mormon a previous pastor of mine's "Everything with God cannot be explained, and if you are at a church were everything can be explained; then the Holy Spirit is not there."

Chapter 5

Jesus Is Our Only Hope

"In him was life: and the life was the light of men.
And the light shineth in darkness; the darkness
comprehended it not"

_____St. John 1:4, 5

It is so easy for society, to blame Jesus for today's host of problems and man's ills. But what I find even more appalling are today's generation mind-set and their disrespect towards God and especially towards Jesus! However, the truth of the matter is, this is not the way God intended for us to respond towards his only Begotten, Son—Jesus, (I John 4:9) for it appears, to me, there has been a breach somewhere between man's covenants with God, to accept His Son or either there "has been a perversion of what things were designed to be!"[32] Especially since today's terrible conditions are a result of, demonic forces that have been set in place, since the beginning of time, and is Satan's sole purpose to cause God's people undue hardships whether to destroy families, communities, and cities, due to this, Christians must realize this is the Devil's way to discourage us and to get us to turn our backs on Jesus! But, Satan's evil plan has failed because "2,000 Catholics from around the world are upset at the rightward turn of the Catholic Church, and showed their dislike by protesting on the 35th anniversary of the late Cardinal John Dearden, former Archbishop."[33] What's more, I found it eye opening that the Catholic Church's members do realize that Jesus 'Is Their Only Hope' because "too many Catholics feel there is no hope"[34] as stated by their organizer: Janet Hauter. Furthermore, I believe this was a show of support and also exhibited their faith in Jesus, for the Catholics "all wore stoles, usually only worn by clergy, to symbolize that all Catholics, and not only its leaders, represent the Church. And they took it a step further, "for on the red stoles they wore, there was a drawing of a dove with the words: "Come Holy Spirit. Fill the hearts of your faithful and kindle in them the fire of your love."[35]

Thinking, "All I can say is oh how the sound of these words, bring joy to my heart and comfort to my soul for Jesus said, *"But the Comforter, which is the Holy Spirit, whom the Father will send in my name, he shall teach you all things, and bring all things to your remembrance, whatever I have said unto you."* (St John 14: 26) Without a doubt, I believe that "Only Jesus can make such a promise to humankind about the Holy Spirit. But, I wondered if Archbishop Vigneron who is loyal to the Pope in Rome believes in the Holy Spirit!" Then the Holy Spirit descended upon read St John 14:1, for this is what the Catholic Church members realizes that their church leaders don't *"Let not your heart be troubled: ye believe in God, believe also in me."* I replied, "Yeah, Lord because the 'Eucharistic Prayer' won't bring them 'Hope' only Jesus can do that!" I wondered, "If they were putting to much emphasis on all the "Hail Mary's" they do—in their communion service!"

On the other hand, a conference held by the Archdiocese expressed a different opinion, stating that the Catholics who took part in the "Eucharistic prayer"[36] were going against the orders of the Archbishop Allen Vigneron, and they were not showing their loyal to Rome. For they felt the Mass led by Rev. Bob Wurm, 78, and contrary to accepted belief, it is frowned upon by the Catholic Church and is viewed as" heretical."[37] In lieu of this, I must say that I agree with participant Robert Livingston, 72, of Berkley, when he expressed concern that "The Church is going backwards," and is guilty of taking the Church back to the days, when believers in Christ were burned at the stake; for not being loyal to men! As I analyzed what I had read in this article, it dawned on me that perhaps the scripture John 1:4, 5 was referring to the Catholic Church as the "light that shineth in darkness" and was stealing the people's hope away—from them! The last two Scriptures the Holy Spirit gave me to share with the members of the Catholic Church's Mass as to the reason, Jesus is their 'only hope' is found in St. John 14:27, *"Peace I leave with you, my peace I Give unto you: not as the world giveth, give I unto you. Let not your heart be troubled, neither let it be afraid."*

Of equally importance, is that "Even the Spirit of truth; whom the world cannot receive, because it seeth him not, neither knoweth him: but ye know him; for he dwelleth with you, and shall be in you." (St. John 14:17) All I could say is that "The Catholic Church and some Evangelical pastors who claim to be your servants Lord, are guilty of not adhering to St John 14:27." And all I can say to them is "Woe." But Jesus said, *"There shall be weeping and gnashing of teeth, when ye shall see Abraham, and Isaac, and Jacob, and all the prophets, in the kingdom of God, and you yourselves thrust out."* (St. Luke 14:28) Because when they could have accepted Jesus as their 'only hope' they denied Him!" Nevertheless, the Lord you told us in St John 15:18-19: *"If the world hates you, ye know that it hated me before if hated you . . . and if ye were of the world, the world would love his own: but because ye are not of this world, therefore the world hateth you."* As for the church leaders in the Church who call themselves my servants, they have gotten what I told my disciples *"Remember the word that I said unto you, The servant is no greater than his Lord. If they have persecuted me, they will also persecute you; if they kept my saying, they will keep your also."* (St. John 15:18-20) As I bid the Holy Spirit good night, for this was heavy on my heart, "Lord, don't the Catholic Church leaders along with Evangelical ministers care that they are causing division in the Body of Christ?" Suddenly the Apostle Paul, a 'true' servant of Jesus Christ added this as an after thought "Now, I beseech you, brethren, mark them which cause divisions and offenses contrary to the doctrine . . . and avoid them." Why the Christian might ask, is because these false teachers "For they that are such serve not our Lord Jesus Christ, but their own belly; and by good words and fair speeches deceive the hearts of the simple." (Romans 16:17-18) I thanked the Apostle Paul, because unlike some pastors whose books I have read, I felt "They were definitely out for themselves and not my Lord and Savior—Jesus Christ!"

Chapter 6

Put on the Whole Armor of God

"Stand therefore, having your loins girt about with truth, and having on the breastplate of righteousness . . ."

_____Ephesians 6:`14

Whether Christians realize it or not, there's a spiritual war waged against us, and it might be coming from a place you might least expect, right from within the walls of the church, and from someone you trust your pastor! It seems, just when the church community though the New Age Movement was dead it has been revived, and has"reinvented itself as the 'New Spirituality' and it will be everything that the Lord Jesus Christ warned would come in his name,"[38] but it is our Lord and Savior, Jesus Christ that Christians owe their salvation too, and we not to confused or mislead, and we must pay serious attention to the Scriptures, for Ephesians 5: 17, 18 admonishes us to "Wherefore be ye not unwise, but understanding what the will of the Lord is . . . but be filled with the Spirit, and you won't be mislead by ministers who are preaching the "panentheistic New Age teaching that God is "in" everything,"[39] this is the reverse, of what Jesus said "Then if man shall say unto you, Lo, here is Christ, or there; believe it not." (Matt. 24:23) Why?

As Christians who are faithful followers of Jesus Christ and heed Jesus words, *"Even the Spirit of truth; whom the world cannot receive, because it seeth him hot, neither knoweth him: but ye know him: for he dwelleth with you, and shall be in you,"* (John 14:17) in lieu of this, "we ought to obey God rather than men." (Acts 5:29) Especially since "Christian leaders who remain in denial about the very real threat of this pervasive spiritual deception that will seriously endanger many who are trusting in their judgment"[40] and instead of setting Christians and not to mention, the unsaved on the path to enter the strait gate which leads to the road of eternal life, they are leading them down the path of destruction that goes; straight to the gates of hell! (Matt. 7:13, 14) Contrary to, popular belief within the church rank and file that the "New Age teachings are taking the church into its New Spirituality,"[41] I agree with author, Warren B. Smith who wrote A "Wonderful" Deception that Pastor "Rich Warren and other Christian leaders fall for New Age schemes rather than exposing them, they will take countless numbers of sincere people down with them, and it will be the blind leading the blind."[42] As I thought about what Warren Smith's words, these pastors reminded me of the priest in Jesus' day, and Jesus had to draws out these "Pharisee ites" as I call them, who are similar to our church leaders today for they also have erred from the truth— that is God's Word, and have reinvented the wheel making up a new religion that reflects man's plans "to redeem society"[43] instead of following God's plan in the Bible, but instead of serving Baal, they have chosen to worship this New Age god! That isn't real either! After I vented, then the Holy Spirit descended upon me and gave me the scripturally correct way He views these supposedly servants of the Lord who have elected not to: heed Christ's Law. "Here is what I have to say*"Whosoever therefore shall break one of these least commandments, and shall teach men so, he shall be called the least in the kingdom of heaven . . ."* (Matthew 5:19) And to address what you said about the 'ities' pastors of your day that talk like the Pharisees in my day, this is my thought about them *"For I say unto you, That* *except your rightheousness shall exceed the righteousness of the scribe and Pharisees, ye shall in no case enter into the kingdom of heaven."* (Matthew 5:20) I thanked the Lord for backing me up, and told him good night.

In this situation, God has not left his people [Believers] powerless; we must heed II Corinthians 10:3-4, "For though we walk in the flesh, we do war after the flesh: (For the weapons of our warfare are not carnal, but mighty through God to the pulling down of strong holds)" demonic or otherwise. But for your spiritual weapons to work you must be in right standing with God and living a righteous life and (submit to God's Will) instead of man's will, and understand the purpose of your spiritual armor that God has given us to ward off the demonic influences that we are being bombarded with in the church, from our pastors without even realizing it! Furthermore the Christian armor that God has given us is explained in Ephesians 6:14-18, "Stand therefore, having your loins girt about with truth, and having on the breastplate of righteousness; . . . Above all, taking the shield of faith, wherewith ye shall be able to quench all the fiery darts of the wicked. And take the helmet of salvation, and the Sword of the Spirit, which is the word of God: Praying always with all prayer and supplication in the Spirit . . ." Thinking about the scriptures above, God has given us a way out, to defend ourselves, "But whoever though, we would have to defend ourselves from God's servants!" The Holy Spirit chimed in *"Many will say to me in that day, Lord, Lord, have we not prophesied in thy name? and in thy name have cast out devils? Only to hear "And then will I profess unto them, I never knew you: depart from me, ye that work iniquity."* (Matthew 7:22, 23)

Thinking I said, "They ministers didn't only cast out devils, they open the doors of the church, for Satan to come in!" Oh well, they won't be hearing "Well done, good and faithful servant or going to heaven" Because they have been wavered between God's Word and fall for the tricks of the god of this world, Satan, I can hear God telling these falling saints same as He told Lucifer,

"Get thee hence" and the only kingdom they will dominate is Hell—along with the Devil and his motley crew!

So you might ask what is it that the Christian needs to understand about the spiritual armor. First of all, it's crucial that Christians take the "Belt of Truth with them everywhere and this includes the church, for the Belt of Truth is our "spiritual mirror that we examine ourselves against is the Word of God, Jesus is the Word and He is the truth,"[44]and helps us to walk the straight instead of the narrow path and is our gauge to whether or not we are: saved or unsaved! Why is this of importance to the Christian? Because "truth can either offend" and causes us to be mislead not the shepherds of God's House for we are in denial"[45] especially when it comes to accepting God's word as truth, and because to this, God commands us to put on our spiritual armor " . . . that ye may be able to withstand in the evil day, and having done all to stand" (Ephesians 6:13) More importantly, to quote Bishop Toney Owens the benefits of accepting the truth is that it brings freedom (John 8:31-32) for Jesus said, "I am the way, the truth and the life: no man cometh unto the Father, but by me." What's more, the good thing about the 'Belt of Truth' is that it also frees Christians from demonic deception and brings and "moves us from righteousness to righteousness"[46] and allows us to keep our right standing with God; instead of man and Satan to accept the New Age Spirituality and their New Age god. There is every reason to conclude, and to quote my Pastor, Supt Tommy C.Vanover I, this "Is like dragging the Blood Stained Banner of Jesus Christ through the mud."

Chapter 7

The Great Commission

"Go therefore and make disciples of all nations, baptizing them in the name of the Father and of the Son and of the Holy Spirit, teaching them to observe all things that I have commanded you . . ."

_____Matthew 28:18-20

The Great Commission found in the Gospel of Matthew, "is one of the most significant passages in the Holy Bible, for it is the last recorded personal instruction given by Jesus to His disciples,"[47] for this command from Jesus is awe-inspiring to Christians because it shows evidence of our faith in Jesus Christ, as indicated in verse 18 above, and more so because, Jesus rein rates that "All authority has been given to Me in heaven and earth,"[48] and if we love Jesus as we claim, Christians recognize that the scripture in verse 18, validates "Christ's omnipotence, and therefore His deity, and if Christians do not believe this statement, complete faith does not exist!"[49]

Yet, it seems to me, that today's leaders in the church are not adhering to Scripture, as it relates to fulfilling God's command to make disciples of men, women and children baptizing them in the name of the 'Father and of the Son and of the Holy Spirit' for this is the missing ingredient of adhering to Jesus' command and is; a vital part of performing the Great Commission! Thinking, "Lord nobody ever mentions the Holy Spirit, especially since a lot of pastors are teaching their people attending worship Pastor Robert Schuller's "hybridized New Age "Christianity,"[50] and he wants to "positivize religion."[51] "Lord, its obvious that Schuller doesn't like the sound of the "un" words like repentance, admit our sins, we are guilty, and I'm afraid that's the complete opposite of what Jesus commands in regards to the Great Commission! And its going against the grain 'Especially when it refers to having faith of a mustard seed." (Matthew 17:20) Thinking I said, "I wonder how Pastor Robert Schuller feels about the Holy Spirit."

Especially since verse 19 in Matthew is equally as important, for "Christ is specially teaching the doctrine of the Trinity to His followers . . . presented in the logical order of Father, Son, and Holy Spirit."[52] What's even sadder, "Is that the 'Son 'is what the Great Commission is all about, and numerous church leaders want to leave Him out of everything." Indeed, this is heartbreaking but true, but pastors and ministers along with Christians "are instructed to teach others about Jesus Christ and the entirety of His Truth, for we can't profess Christ as Savior and Lord while rejecting certain of His teachings."[53] Suddenly the Holy Spirit descended upon me, for I needed to hear the Lord's take on this and I was given this scripture in the Bible to look up I John 4:1. "Beloved, believe not every spirit, but try the spirits whether they are of God: because many false prophets are gone out into the world." My only thought was because of my profound faith in Jesus Christ as my Lord and Savior, it is my saintly duty to heed his command and undertake the Great Commission challenge for this is my personal commitment to Jesus that I belonged to Him and would not deter from his teachings to follow some pastor that can't even save himself—let alone me!" The Holy Spirit was pleased with my response and told me to read I John 4:4-5, "Ye are of God, little children, and have overcome them: because greater is he that is in you, than he that is in the world, . . . they are of the world: therefore speak they of the world, and the world heareth them." That's too bad for "Like God kicked Satan, that ole Antichrist out of heaven along with his harebrained followers, these same church leaders will spend eternal bound in hells bottomless pit, for they have erred from the truth and have; accepted Satan's half truths and lies!" In lieu of this, and as food for the thought, Christians who are Jesus disciples must heed these words "In the Great Commission, Jesus calls every Christian to step out in faith and spread the Good News"[54] for then, we will being what Jesus expects us and is more than a command; its an honor—to be of service to God!

So, the question Christians should be asking is "How do we become "fisher of men"[55] to follow Jesus command to do the Great Commission by spreading joy, instead of more bad news! But before Christians can use the power given to us by the Holy Spirit, they must preach the Gospel that we back up to be genuine and true, for this is proof of God's love towards those that are lost, and who are looking for: hope in a broken world! Due to this, Christians are to become 'fisher of men' (Matthew 4:18, 19) same as when Jesus called the two brother Simon (called Peter) and Andrew, but Jesus took it a step further and showed them how to use their experience as fishermen to evangelize and to preach the Gospel to the sea of humanity bringing the lost, unrepentant, and unbalanced to Jesus! And one of the ways Christians can accomplish this goal is to take up Jesus' Cross understanding that He died, in order to stop the Devil from snatching our souls and thrusting them into the fiery furnace of hell. For Jesus understood what we didn't that since the beginning of time Satan, that ole Devil goal is and always has been is to see humankind drowning in the sea of un forgiveness without any chance of being pardon and; hope cease to exist! But thanks to Jesus, he has already laid the foundation, for He has conquered death and overcame man's fiercest enemy! So Christians can take up the baton and run the race knowing that we our triumphant over the Devil, and he has lost the battle for our souls, because our faith in Jesus and to fulfill the Great Commission is stronger than the roar of a cowardly lion! In addition, I agree wholeheartedly with Bishop Tony Owens that "true knowledge of, and in faith, our risen Savior, will give us the passion and desire to go fishing for souls." Why you might ask? because this was the driving force for the Twelve Disciples picked personally by Jesus as a result, of their faith and believing that Jesus liberated us from death! Because of this, Christians same as the disciples must heed the Scripture in Luke 12:4-5 explains why, "And I say unto you my friends, Be not afraid of them that kill the body, and after that have no more power to cast into hell; yea, I say unto you, Fear him." All I could say is that "The demons tremble at the Name of Jesus and whether he admits or not, so does Satan." The Holy Spirit appeared saying read "Hebrew 4:12, for the Word of God "is quick and powerful, sharper than any twoedged sword, that pierces even to the dividing asunder of soul and spirit, and the joints and morrow, and is a discerner of the thoughts and the intents of the heart." I replied, "That's cutting edge sharp, Lord." But because of you Lord giving up your valued blood and us following your command to do the Great Commission, the battle for ours souls won't be ever ending and we won't have to fear that Satan is always on the hunt for lost souls! And this was the Holy Spirit's last words to me, "Be not deceived, for Satan can appear as an angel of light—especially if you don't believe and accept Me!" I replied, "But I do Lord and it's your blood that covers and protects— me!" As a final thought, the Lord told me to read Matthew 5:13, for shows how man has fallen off the spiritual band wagon of Christianity, *Ye are the salt of the earth: but if the salts have lost his savor, wherewith shall it be salted? it is thenceforth good for nothing, but to be cast out, and to be trodden under the foot of men.* Thinking to me, "Why would mankind listen to pastors and ministers whose words are none and void—talking and saying nothing!" And the Holy Spirit came to me for the last time to night and told me to read Matthew 13:1 and this will answer your question "Though I speak with the tongues of men and of angels, and have not charity, I am become as sounding brass, or a tinkling cymbal."

Chapter 8

The Catholic Church's Communion: Worships another Jesus

"This cup is the new testament in my blood: this do ye, as oft as ye drink it, in remembrance of me."

_____I Corinthians 11: 25

For it's as if Paul is speaking to us through the winds of time, for he realized that Satan's false gospel and evil spirit would not only compromise our faith in Jesus, but our salvation is also at stake! About this, "these Spirits are waging a relentless war against all of humanity, to the world it is just the way that things are, but to Christians, it is a perversion of God's intended purposes."[56] For Satan's plan is that Christians accept and worship the Eucharist Jesus, clearly, this is entirely different from what the Scriptures' teaches about salvation, after all, our faith is built on Jesus salvation on the Cross of Calvary. As it stands, Satan's plan to deceive the elect started with Eve, in the Garden of Eden and still holds true today, but his goal is to defrock the High Priest of them all, Jesus Christ, and authors Roger Oakland with Jim Tetlow in their book *Another Jesus* states that "current trends indicate we may be headed down a similar pathway leading towards a strong deception that has the potential of not just deceiving the whole world"[57] — but the Body of Christ too! Similarity, scores of Christians Christ Jesus' followers believe otherwise, for there is no other god, whose salvation can compete or take the place of Jesus' salvation, for He is the only way, truth and the life! Not to mention, the Eucharist isn't mention once in the Scriptures for Jesus laid the groundwork for those seeking salvation, and Jesus humanity's only hope, because of this, I Corinthians 3:11, clearly states, "For other foundation can no man lay, that is laid, which is Jesus Christ" and "genuine conversion to Christ is not a mere human act of calling Christ our Savior . . . but genuine conversion is a divine act by which a Spirit of sonship is made to dwell in our heart."[58] Despite, what Christians believe the Lord's Supper or communion in the Catholics' service is contrary to the command our Lord Jesus requested his followers to do in Remembrance of Me, according to authors Oakland and Tetlow "The Eucharist (i.e. Transubstantiation) is a Catholic term for communion when the bread and the wine are supposed to become the very body and blood of Jesus Christ."[59] Furthermore, Oakland goes on to explain that "these transformed elements are placed in what is called a monstrance and can be worshipped as if worshipping Jesus Himself."[60] So whether Christians realize it or not, we are in the midst of a spiritual battle, and Satan is competing with God for our minds and unquestionably our souls, and we must be aware of his deceitful plan, to keep us from hearing the Good News of the Gospel! Certainly, Satan's goal to get Christians to believe and accept another gospel, another Jesus tricking us into believing in "an experiential form of Christianity centered on the miraculous instead of an understanding of the Gospel."[61] Because of this, Christians should not be swayed Satan for Ephesians 4:14, rein rated to Christ's flock" That we henceforth be no more children, tossed to and fro, and carried about with every wind of doctrine by human cunning with cleverness in the techniques of deceit." For this reason, the Apostle Paul forewarned Christians to heed II Corinthians 11:1-4, "For if he that cometh preacheth another Jesus, whom we have not preached, or if ye receive another spirit, which ye have not accepted, ye might well bear with him." I was confused and asked the Lord, "How can this be?" For a monstrance is kept on display on an altar, chills ran down my spine, just the thought of a 'mere' man (priest) having the authority to perform such a sacred act that to me, was solely Jesus Christ's ultimate act of love to break the yoke of Satan's control on humankind— and keep us from being thrust into hell evermore!

"Sure I am upset, because to me, I will not be part of a pagan ritual. For that's not what I believe in a communion service worshipping a god in an urn!" And the more I thought about the purpose an urn serves, I thought, "It's as if Satan wants us to believe Jesus Christ is dead and has been cremated! But my Lord and Savior is alive, even the stone the Roman guards put at Jesus' tomb couldn't hold Him!" Again the Holy Spirit descended upon me "Wanda read Jude 1:2-4, those of us who have received Jesus' free gift of salvation, must contend for the faith because "there are certain men crept in unawares, who were before of old ordained to this condemnation ungodly men, turning the grace of our God into lasciviousness and denying the only Lord God, and our Lord Jesus Christ." Finally I was understood what the Holy Spirit was telling me, which is the question Christians should be asking is whose salvation plan is misguiding is it Jesus', Satan's or the: Catholic Church's?

But lest we forget, Jesus' plan of salvation is humanity's only hope, for I Corinthians 4:11 explains why, "For other foundation can no man lay, that is laid, which is Jesus Christ." That's it, "Christ Jesus is nothing like Baal, and Satan wants to turn my Savior, Jesus— into a modern day scapegoat. But it won't fly because Christians refuse to be apart of the Judas Iscariot fan club! "What's more, the Eucharist is linked to salvation although to me, it turns Jesus' free gift of salvation into a blasphemous, unorthodox, and disrespectful ritual. Tears streaming down my face, I said, "Lord this is just plain evil."

The Lord reminded me saying, "Wanda, remember I told you in my word that "there shall be false teachers among you, who privily shall bring in damnable heresies, even denying the

Lord that, bought them, by reason of whom the way of truth shall be evil spoken of" (2 Peter 2:1-2) I replied. "Yes, Lord but it saddens me the lies that ole devil, Satan is putting out about you." The Lord just kept giving me scriptures in God's Word to reassure me and the Lord reminded me again, "For we walk by faith, not by sight." (2 Corinthians 5:7) Then the Holy Spirit descended upon me Wanda, "God is not a man, that he should lie; neither the son of man." (Numbers 23:19) In bidding me good night the Holy Spirit gave this last scripture in Colossians 1:13 –14, for it is Jesus "Who hath delivered us from the power of darkness, and hath translated us into the kingdom of his dear Son: In whom we have redemption through his blood."

Furthermore," approximately 2.1 billion"[62] Christians, far-reaching and around the globe believe God's Word, the Bible to be true and unconditional accept Jesus Christ, as our Lord and Savior, for no other god, can measure up to him! Because of this, Christians worship and are faithful to the historical Jesus, and in no way would we swap Christ Jesus nor serve 'another Jesus' willingly, especially a make-believe Jesus that Satan plans to use to deceive Christian, so that are faith will be in vain! Instead, we have chosen to listen to the apostle Paul, that unless we worship and believe in Christ Jesus the authentic Savior otherwise "our faith will be in vain." In lieu of those infamous words, Christians identify and acknowledge God's only Begotten Son, Jesus as the 'true' Savior and the only one, who is worth worshipping, because Jesus is the only person that can ensure our salvation! So whether the Eucharist, to quote Roger Oakland and Jim Tetlow *(a former Catholic)* is the "new evangelization" surfacing in Catholic Churches globally, without a doubt, Christians followers of Jesus Christ worship whom the scriptures point too, adhere to Roman 8:38-39," For I am persuaded, that neither death, nor life, nor angels, nor principalities, nor powers, nor things present, nor things to come, nor height, nor depth, nor any other creature, shall be able to separate us from the love of God, which is in Christ Jesus our Lord." Especially as it relates to the church "redressing the historical injustices"[63] that Jesus endured 2,000 years and is still subjected to today! Indeed, Satan's false teachers have infiltrated the Church of Rome and are laying the groundwork for Satan's political and social agenda the; revival of the One World Church, and they have chosen to denounce Christ Jesus for the Eucharist. But is it worth it Saints, to throw your inheritance that Jesus promises us, to serve a lesser god who can't even; save humanity. About this, ask yourselves what hope do we have in worshipping a different Jesus, whose plan for salvation is entirely the reverse of the 'real' Jesus' plan for salvation, and combines "Jesus plus works"[64] in the salvation equation, and is the complete opposite of "justification by faith in Christ alone,"[65] "But how can this be? He's so much like Baal, who didn't answer his followers' prayers either, and they cut themselves and spilled their blood on the ground hoping to conjure him up—but nothing worked. It's no wonder, Believers heed the words of a true disciple of Jesus, the Apostle Paul in Roman 8:15, "For ye have not received the spirit of bondage again to fear; but ye have received the Spirit of adoption, whereby we cry, "Abba, Father," is way better than losing our salvation to worship a bogus god that can't save us or hear our cries! So why anybody would chose to partake in a communion service and worship, not only another Jesus but a different spirit masquerading as the 'true' Savior! In like manner, Jesus Christ is the only one who can save souls and keeps us from rotting in Hades! So how is it that Satan our enemy, causes the faithful to question Jesus' creditability, especially when it comes to salvation, and the church of all places, is following in Satan's footsteps; putting Jesus Christ on trial, the founder of the Church and the finisher of the faith! More importantly, Jesus is quick to forgive us, when we repent of our sins and ask for forgiveness, but Christians must make a choice who they will serve Christ Jesus, the one and only Redeemer or the Eucharist, for Jesus Christ salvation has stood the test of time, and proves that Satan is a liar and a master illusionist. Because of this lest we forget, Christians are warned to be on the look out for another

Jesus, and to "contend for the faith" (Jude 1:3-4) for "there are certain men crept in unawares, who were before of old ordained to this condemnation ungodly men, turning the grace of our God into lasciviousness and denying the only God, and our Lord Jesus Christ." Thinking to myself, "Its obvious Satan only cares about himself, and he wants to see Christians' burn in the lake of fire with him and his false teachers! So ask yourself Saints, whose message of salvation is deadly and misleading? So why should we worship and accept the Eucharist's dry bones salvation, (Ezekiel 37:5) especially who wasn't murdered for crime he didn't commit, or left half dead to hang on the on the Cross with the rays of the sun scotching his weather beaten body, who didn't sacrifice an ounce of his blood dripping painstakingly slowly from the excruciating pain of the nails that were impaled into his hands and feet! Even through all the pain and suffering Jesus Christ when through including being spat on and treated like a common criminal, he still had compassion for us, and our best is like filthy rags! Yet, Jesus mustered up enough strengthen to whisper the words "Forgive them Father, for they know not what they do," (St. Luke 23:34) and this is the Jesus story that Christians; hold steadfast too!

Despite Satan's plan to dupe the people of God into believing in 'another Jesus' and another gospel, and to make Christ Jesus a scapegoat in the world's eyes, it's really the Eucharist, a mock Christ, who is going to usher in a lot of pain and suffering to the elect, all because we have chosen to believe Satan, who is a troublemaker and illusionist! For this reason, Bible believing Christians accept and believe Christ Jesus promises to the faithful, that He is the only God who can break give us his free gift of salvation; keeping us from pining away in hell eternally. What's more, how is it that Satan our enemy can get Christians to follow in his footsteps to worship a false deity, over Jesus Christ, our Lord and Savior! So, Beloved will you serve Jesus Christ or the Eucharist, in my opinion, who gives the outward appearance of being sacred, but can't set the captives free! There is every indication; that false leaders in the church have been influenced by demonic spirits and have chosen "to drag the blood stained banner of Jesus Christ through the mud,"[66] and to the Roman Catholic Church leadership, I wonder if they are adhering to Revelation 22:18-19:

"FOR I TESTIFY UNTO EVERY MAN THAT BEARETH THE WORDS OF THE PROPHECY OF THIS BOOK. IF ANY MAN SHALL ADD UNTO THESE THINGS, GOD SHALL ADD UNTO HIM THE PLAGUES THAT ARE WRITTEN IN THIS BOOKGOD SHALL ADD UNTO THESE . . . AND IF ANY MAN SHALL TAKE AWAY FROM THE WORDS OF THE BOOK OF THIS PROPHECY, GOD SHALL TAKE WAY HIS PART OUT OF THE BOOK OF LIFE."

And these are my last words, "Woe to these false teachers, for God's wrath is upon them. And all I can say for our sake is "Come quickly Lord Jesus, for Satan's plan is to deceive the followers of Jesus Christ to worship the Eucharist who, can not save us!"

Chapter 9

Conclusion

As we can see, our enemy, Satan not only wants to steal our self-assurance but our belief in Jesus Christ, but his desire is for Christians to forsake our Lord and Savior, Jesus by deceiving us to accept the Eucharist, an end time deity that worships the Antichrist, whose goal is to finish what he started in the Garden of Eden, to destroy God's people that He created in His image and likeness; instead of the rebellious archangel, Lucifer! Because of Satan's ultimate plan to reduce the human race to nothing, Jesus Christ has chosen to stand in proxy for us, and once and for all, get rid of the most oppressive tyrant; the world has ever known! It's no surprise, that even in the prophet's Ezekiel's day, that God was looking for "an intercessor or someone who would stand proxy for the land"[67] but there no one to be found, or who could stand up to Satan. But, the Divine Intercessor, Christ Jesus will fight mankind's fiercest enemy and Ezekiel 22:30-31 reads, "And I sought for a man among them, that should make up the hedge, and stand in the gap before me for the land; . . . but I found none. Therefore have I poured out mine indignation upon them: I will consume them with the fire of my wrath," Suddenly my thoughts turned to the 2nd Coming of Christ Jesus, "Satan, you and the Antichrist--- are toast!"

In lieu of God standing in proxy for unrepentant sinners who have chosen to turn their backs on Him, and in spite of their unfaithfulness, I am dedicating this poem to my Lord and Savior,

Christ Jesus. He has stood in proxy for me numerous times, what about you?

Will You Stand In the Gap For Jesus?

Will you stand in the gap for Jesus?
    for He stood in the gap for you;
    even when you rejected Him—
    He let his love— for us shine through

Will you stand in the gap for Jesus?
    He took a thousand lashes;
    to show His love—
    for you;

Will you stand in the gap for Jesus?
    He was crucified;
    Because He told the truth,

Will you stand in the gap for Jesus?
    Because He went to Calvary;
    to save us from the Antichrist—
    whose plan;
    is to crucify— us too!

Endnotes

1   Bell, Rob, A Book About Heaven, Hell And The Fate Of Every Person Who Ever Lived (New York, NY: Harper Collins Publishers, 2011), p,. viii, PREFACE.

2   www.Battle4Truth.com   (John Macarthur's quote take off website)

3   www.wikipedia.org/wiki/political correctness (Section on Right-winged political correctness)

4   Oakland, Roger with Jim Tetlow, Another Jesus? the Eucharistic Christ and the new evangelization (Silverton, Oregon: Lighthouse Trails Publishing, 2004) Catholic term for communion and was taken from back cover of book

5   http://cnview.com/churches_today/chapter_2_truth_about_the_church. htm accessed on 05/27/2011

6   http://mountainretreatorg.net/bible/sola_scriptura.shtml moved accessed on 05/27/2011

7   Ibid.,

8   Ibid.,

9   http://www.cbsnews.com/stories/2007/10/11/60minutes/main3358652_page3.shtm accessed on 05/27/2011

10   Ibid.,

11   http://mountainretreatorg.net/bible/sola_scriptura.shtml

12   Ibid.,

13   http://www.angelfire.com/la2/prophet1/rgstair01.html moved accessed on 05/27/2011

14   Ibid.,

15   http://www.cbsnews.com/stories/2007/10/11/60minutes/main3358652_page3.shtm accessed on 05/27/2011

16   Ibid.,

17   http://www.cuttingedge.org/news/n1171.cfm accessed 05/25/2011

18   Ibid.,

19   Ibid.,

20   http://www.mountainretreatorg.net/bible/sola_scriptura.shtml accessed 05/25/2011

21   Ibid.,

22   Ibid.,

23   Ibid.,

24   Sceniorette Owens, The Dynamics Of Prayer, (Valley Stream, NY: House of David Ministries, Inc., 2009), p.28

25   Ibid., p. 27

26   All Scriptures taken from the King James Version The Open Bible (Unless otherwise noted)

27   Rob Bell, Love Wins: A Book About Heaven, Hell, And the Fate Of Every Person Who Ever Lived, (New York, NY: HarperCollins, and HarperOne of HarperCollins Publishers, 2011), p. viii Preface

28   Ibid., p. x Preface

29   http://www.mountainretreatorg.net/bible/sola_scriptura.shtml accessed on 05/25/2011

30   http://simplyagape.blogspot.com/2008/09/rob-bell-exposed. html

31   King James Version, The Open Bible, (Royal Publishers), p.1109

32   Tony Owens, How To Engage In Spiritual Warfare Victoriously, (Valley Stream, NY: House of David Ministries, Inc., 2008), p.23

33   http://www.freep.com.com/article/20110612/News05/110612013/1001/rss01 accessed on 6/11/2011

34   Ibid.,

35   Ibid.,

36   Ibid.,

37   Ibid.,

38   Warren B. Smith, A Wonderful Deception: The Further New Age Implications of the Emerging/Purpose Driven Movement, (Eureka, Montana: Lighthouse Trials Publishing, 2009), p.12 Preface

39   Ibid., p.16

40   Ibid., p. 29

41   Ibid., p. 28

42   Ibid., p. 29

43   Ibid., p. 24

44   Tony Owens, How To Engage In Spiritual Warfare Victoriously, (Valley Stream, NY: House of David Ministries, Inc., 2008), p. 16

45   Ibid., p. 16

46   Ibid., .p.17

47   http://www.allaboutjesuschrist.org/thegreat-great-commission.htm accessed on 6/13/2011

48   Ibid.,

49   Ibid.,

50 Warren B. Smith, A "Wonderful" Deception: The Further New Age Implication of the Emerging/Purpose Driven Movement, (Eureka, Montana: Lighthouse Trails Publishing, 2009), p. 37

51 Ibid., p.38

52 http://www.allaboutjesuschrist.org/thegreat-great-commission.htm accessed on 6/13/2011

53 Ibid.,

54 Ibid.,

55 Bishop Tony Owens, Kingdom Character: Discipleship IV, (Valley Stream, NY: House of David Ministries, Inc., 2008) p. 1

56 Tony Owens, How To Engage in Spiritual Warfare Victoriously, (Valleystream, NY: House of David Ministries, Inc,2008),p.1

57 Roger Oakland With Jim Tetlow, Another Jesus the eucharistic Christ and the new evangelization, (Silverton, Oregon: Lighthouse Trails Publishing, 2007) , p. 11.

58 http://www.soundofgrace.com/piper83/082183m.htm, moved accessed on 05/10/2011

59 Ibid. (Took quote from the back cover of book)

60 Ibid. (Took quote from back cover of book)

61 Ibid., p. 12

62 http://www.adherents.com/Religions By Adherents. html, accessed on 05/10/2011

63 http://www.answers.com/topic/political- correctness

64 Roger Oakland with Jim Tetlow, Another Jesus? the Eucharistic Christ and the new evangelization, (Silverton, Oregon: Lighthouse Trails Publishing, 2007), p. 20

65 Roger Oakland with Jim Tetlow, Another Jesus? the Eucharistic Christ and the new evangelization, (Silverton, Oregon: Lighthouse Trails Publishing, 2007), Quote taken from back cover of book

66 Quote taken from my Pastor Tommy C. Vanover I

67 Tony Owens, How To Engage in Spiritual Warfare Victoriously, (Valleystream, NY: House of David Ministries, Inc, 2008), p.30